Significant Battles of the American Revolution

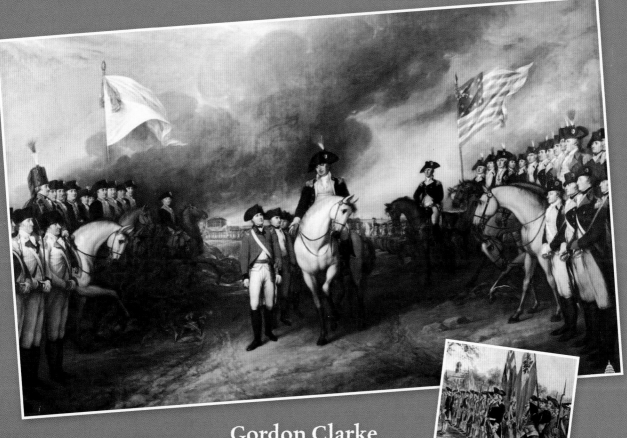

Gordon Clarke

CRABTREE
Publishing Company
www.crabtreebooks.com

Understanding The American Revolution

Author: Gordon Clarke
Publishing plan research and development:
Sean Charlebois, Reagan Miller
Crabtree Publishing Company
Editors: Leslie Jenkins, Janet Sweet, Lynn Peppas
Proofreaders: Lisa Slone, Kelly McNiven
Editorial director: Kathy Middleton
Production coordinator: Shivi Sharma
Cover design: Samara Parent, Margaret Amy Salter
Photo research: Nivisha Sinha
Maps: Paul Brinkdopke
Production coordinator and prepress technician: Samara Parent
Print coordinator: Katherine Berti

Written, developed, and produced by Planman Technologies

Cover: *The Death of General Mercer* at the Battle of Princeton by artist John Trumbull. The battle was a victory for George Washington.

Title page: (main) A painting by John Trumbull shows British officer Lord Cornwallis surrendering at Yorktown, ending the American Revolution.
(bottom) An American soldier under the command of General Washington at Cambridge.

Photographs and Reproductions
Front Cover: John Trumbull/Wikimedia Commons (b), Shutterstock (t); Title Page: Architect of the Capitol (t); Library of Congress (b); Table of Contents: Library of Congress; Domenick D'Andrea / The National Guard; Introduction: Library of Congress; Chapter 1: Library of Congress; Chapter 2: Library of Congress; Chapter 3: Library of Congress; Chapter 4: Library of Congress; Page 4: Library of Congress (b); Page 5: Library of Congress; Page 9: Library of Congress; Page 10: Library of Congress; Page 11: Domenick D'Andrea / The National Guard; Page 14: Library of Congress; Page 15: Library of Congress; Page 16: ©The Protected Art Archive / Alamy / IndiaPicture; Page 17: Library of Congress; Page 18: Library of Congress; Page 19: Library of Congress; Page 20: Library of Congress; Page 21: Library of Congress; Page 22: wikimedia commons; Page 24: Library of Congress; Page 26: Library of Congress; Page 27: Architect of the Capitol; Page 30: Library of Congress; Page 32: Library of Congress (t); Library of Congress (b); Page 33: Library of Congress; Page 35: Library of Congress; Page 36: ©Classic Image / Alamy / IndiaPicture (t); Don Troiani / The National Guard (b); Page 37: ©The Art Gallery Collection / Alamy / IndiaPicture; Page 39: Library of Congress; Page 40: Christoff / Shutterstock;
(t = top, b = bottom, l = left, c= center, r = right, bkgd = background, fgd = foreground)

Library and Archives Canada Cataloguing in Publication

Clarke, Gordon, 1965-
    Significant battles of the American Revolution / Gordon Clarke.

(Understanding the American Revolution)
Includes bibliographical references and index.
Issued also in electronic format.
ISBN 978-0-7787-0817-9 (pbk.).--ISBN 978-0-7787-0806-3 (bound)

    1. United States--History--Revolution, 1775-1783--Campaigns--Juvenile literature. I. Title. II. Series: Understanding the American Revolution (St. Catharines, Ont.)

E230.C53 2013   j973.3'3   C2013-900244-8

Library of Congress Cataloging-in-Publication Data

CIP available at Library of Congress

Crabtree Publishing Company
www.crabtreebooks.com   1-800-387-7650

Printed in Canada/022013/BF20130114

Published in Canada
Crabtree Publishing
616 Welland Ave.
St. Catharines, Ontario
L2M 5V6

Published in the United States
Crabtree Publishing
PMB 59051
350 Fifth Avenue, 59th Floor
New York, New York 10118

Published in the United Kingdom
Crabtree Publishing
Maritime House
Basin Road North, Hove
BN41 1WR

Published in Australia
Crabtree Publishing
3 Charles Street
Coburg North
VIC 3058

TABLE *of* CONTENTS

Introduction
From Frustration to Resistance | From Protests to Organized Rebellion | From Rebellion to War

4

1

The War Ignites in New England
The Ride of Paul Revere | The Battle of Lexington | The Battle of Concord | The Battle of Bunker (Breed's) Hill | The Siege of Boston | The Battle of Quebec

8

2

The Fight for the Middle Colonies
Battles for New York | The Battle of Trenton | The Battle of Princeton | The Battle of Ticonderoga | Turning Point: Saratoga | The Impact of Saratoga | Pennsylvania & Valley Forge

18

3

The War at Sea
Privateers Support the Patriots | The Continental Navy | France Supports America at Sea

31

4

The South and Yorktown
Savannah and Charleston Seized | The Battles in the Carolinas | Endgame: Yorktown | After the Battles

34

Glossary, 42 | Timeline, 44 | Further Reading and Websites, 45 | Bibliography, 46 | Index, 47

Introduction

American militia

The American Revolutionary War grew out of bitter frustration between the American colonies and Great Britain. By 1774, colonial resentment of British taxes came to a boil, and angry colonists openly protested the British government.

From Frustration to Resistance

For 150 years, the people of the American colonies had been mostly on their own. British rule over them had been loose, and **representative government** had thrived. That began to change after the French and Indian War. Great Britain needed money to pay off their war debts, so **Parliament** tightened its control over the colonies. Britain increased taxes and placed new taxes on the colonies. The colonists pushed back harder with each new set of British restrictions. Great Britain stationed troops in Boston, which had become a hotbed of **resistance**.

From Protests to Organized Rebellion

Instead of an organized army of their own, the colonists had established **militias**. These were groups of armed citizens, who could be called on to act as soldiers if necessary. The youngest and most physically capable militia members—nicknamed "minutemen"—were supposed to respond to a call within a moment's notice. The British had counted on these Patriot militias to be loyal to Britain, but that was not always the case.

Taunting and violence frequently broke out between British troops and the colonists in Boston. Fearing a possible rebellion, the British began to **confiscate** the colonists' weapons. This action caused the Battles of Lexington and Concord. The colonists did not have the formal military training of the British army. However, they fought in large numbers with determination and creative **tactics**.

From Rebellion to War

By 1776, the rebellion had turned into a war for independence. After the colonists suffered military defeats at Bunker Hill and in New York, they focused on developing skills and resources to defend their new country. The colonies' military strength grew, first in the North and then through the South. Patriot victories, like the Battles of Trenton and Saratoga, became more common.

An **alliance** with France in 1778 provided the colonies with money, weapons, troops, and warships. The French navy and raiding Patriot **privateers** hurt Britain's efforts to move troops and supplies. British forces were reduced to occupying small coastal ports in the face of a growing enemy army. Eventually, the British task of defending a position so far from home became too difficult. In 1781, Britain's **surrender** at Yorktown marked the end of the battles of the American Revolutionary War.

The war at sea

What Do You Know!

Before the Revolutionary War, from 1768–1772, the colonies' four largest cities, Philadelphia, New York, Boston, and Charleston, sailed 138,000 tons (125,000 metric tons) of goods to Britain every year.

The Colonies are in open and avowed rebellion.

—Great Britain's King George III, 1774

Hudson's Bay Company

Nova Scotia

Province of Quebec

Massachusetts

claimed by New York and New Hampshire

New Hampshire

Boston

Massachusetts

New York

Rhode Island

Connecticut

Pennsylvania

New York

New Jersey

Philadelphia

Baltimore

Delaware

Maryland

Virginia

Indian Reserve

Spanish Louisiana

North Carolina

South Carolina

ATLANTIC OCEAN

Georgia

Charleston

West Florida

East Florida

	British Territory
	Thirteen Colonies (British)
	Spanish Territory
●	major city
– –	Proclamation Line of 1763*

0   125   250 miles

0   125   250 kilometers

Gulf of Mexico

*This line shows the farthest west British settlers were allowed to go. The rest of the land was reserved for Native Americans.

North America before the Revolutionary War

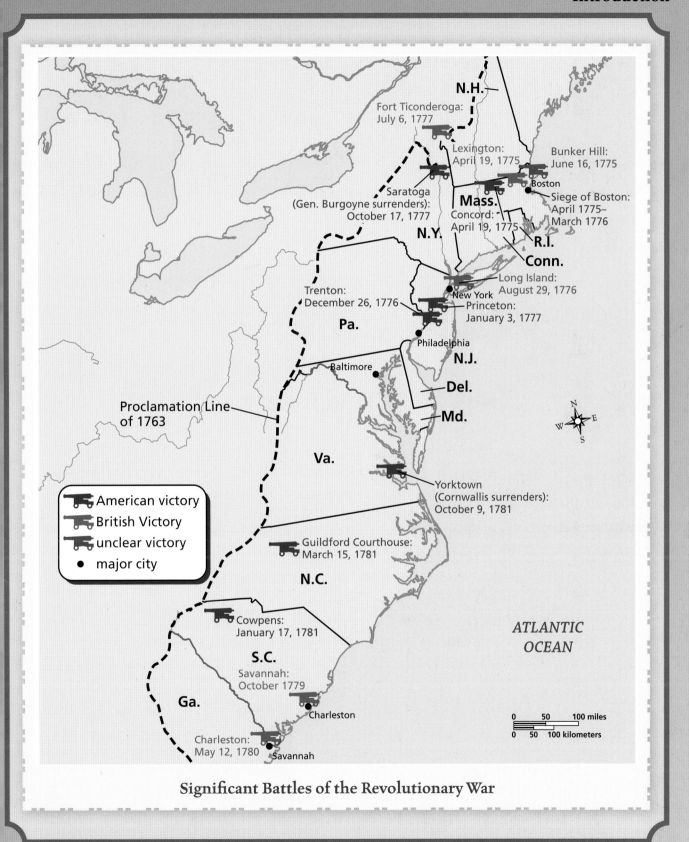

N.H.

Fort Ticonderoga:
July 6, 1777

Lexington:
April 19, 1775

Bunker Hill:
June 16, 1775

Boston

Siege of Boston:
April 1775–
March 1776

Saratoga
(Gen. Burgoyne surrenders):
October 17, 1777

Mass.

Concord:
April 19, 1775

N.Y.

R.I.

Conn.

Long Island:
August 29, 1776

Trenton:
December 26, 1776

New York

Princeton:
January 3, 1777

Pa.

Philadelphia

N.J.

Baltimore

Del.

Proclamation Line
of 1763

Md.

Va.

Yorktown
(Cornwallis surrenders):
October 9, 1781

American victory
British Victory
unclear victory
major city

Guildford Courthouse:
March 15, 1781

N.C.

ATLANTIC
OCEAN

Cowpens:
January 17, 1781

S.C.

Savannah:
October 1779

Ga.

Charleston

Charleston:
May 12, 1780

Savannah

0   50   100 miles
0   50   100 kilometers

Significant Battles of the Revolutionary War

The War Ignites in New England

Major Events
1775

April 19
Battles of Lexington and Concord; war begins in the north

April 19, 1775 – March 17, 1776
Siege of Boston

June 16
Battle of Bunker (Breed's) Hill

December 31
Battle of Quebec

After 150 years of British settlement and rule, the New England colonies rebelled against Great Britain. The other colonies soon joined, but the fight started in New England.

The Ride of Paul Revere

After the British army closed the port of Boston in 1774, Paul Revere organized a group of men to keep a close watch on the British army's movements. His group arranged a warning system in preparation for an attack from Britain. They would let Boston's citizens and militia know how the army intended to cross the Charles River in its attack. If British troops chose the land route over the river, Revere's men would light one lantern in the steeple of Boston's North Church. If the army chose the water route across the river, two lanterns would be lit. This resulted in the famous line "one if by land, two if by sea."

On April 18, 1775, Paul Revere and William Dawes raced to warn the Patriot leaders. The British were moving across the river toward Lexington. Revere and Dawes took different routes to improve the chances that at least one would arrive without being captured. While they rode, they informed other Patriot militias that the British were on the way.

> *To arms, to arms! The British are coming, the British are coming!*
>
> —Paul Revere, 1775

Revere arrived in Lexington shortly before Dawes and informed the Patriot leaders. When Revere and Dawes left for Concord, they were stopped by a British roadblock. The men scattered, but Revere was captured just outside Lexington. Revere convinced the soldiers that the town of Lexington was preparing to fight. Hearing the sounds of gunfire and bells ringing in the town, the British soldiers decided to release Revere and return to Boston to warn their commanders.

The Battle of Lexington

General Thomas Gage was the commander of the British troops in New England. He was ordered by the British government to regain control of the colonies. Gage received information that the rebelling colonists had hidden a large supply of weapons in the town of Concord. On the afternoon of April 18, 1775, Gage ordered Colonel Francis Smith to take 700 soldiers with him to confiscate the colonists' weapons.

Raising the Alarm

With the help of spies, the colonists received word of the British orders even before Gage did. As a result, the colonists had already moved their major supply of weapons from Concord to nearby towns ten days earlier. That evening, Paul Revere and several others rode out of Boston to warn the Patriot leaders of the coming attack.

People in the War

Paul Revere

Paul Revere was a lifelong Bostonian. His father was a silversmith, and Revere learned this trade as well. He was an important supporter of the independence movement in Boston. He even participated in the Boston Tea Party in 1773. During the war, Revere commanded Boston's harbor defenses. After the war, he returned to his life as a silversmith until his death in 1818.

Paul Revere's Ride April 18–19, 1775	
10:00 PM	Revere leaves Boston
11:00 PM	Revere warns Charleston (Mass.) of Britain's plan to attack
11:30 PM	Revere reaches Medford
12:05 AM	Revere reaches Lexington
1:00 AM	Revere stopped by British roadblock on way to Concord; Revere released
4:30 AM	Revere helps Samuel Adams and John Hancock flee Lexington
5:00 AM	Revere witnesses fighting on Lexington Green

The British on the Move

The British soldiers started their trip in the late evening, hoping to arrive before the colonists could react. Once it was dark, they began crossing the Charles River. The crossing was done in a clumsy manner. The boats they used could not reach the opposite side. The soldiers had to climb out of the boats and into the water with their gear and supplies. They lost time and the element of surprise. The British soldiers had to continue their march in muddy shoes and soggy uniforms. As they marched, they could hear the alarms being raised ahead of them.

The British knew they would not surprise anyone in Concord. Colonel Smith sent Major John Pitcairn ahead to Concord along with some of his troops. They had to pass through the town of Lexington to get to Concord. Pitcairn's soldiers entered the town of Lexington at sunrise on April 19. They were met by 77 minutemen and over 100 spectators.

Battle of Lexington

The Shot Heard 'Round the World

Neither group knew how to respond to the other. In the confusion, the minutemen began to withdraw. Then a shot rang out. It was never clear who fired it, but it triggered the beginning of the war. The British soldiers opened fire on the minutemen and charged them with **bayonets**, killing eight men and injuring another ten. When Colonel Smith arrived with the rest of the British troops, he halted the battle and ordered his soldiers to continue their march toward Concord.

> "
> *The flame [of rebellion] is kindled and like lightening it catches from soul to soul. . . .*
>
> —Abigail Adams
> "

The Battle of Concord

Patriot militia members from the surrounding areas began to arrive in Concord. They had heard news of shots being fired in Lexington. A group of about 250 minutemen marched out of Concord, led by Colonel James Barrett. The plan was to stop the British before they arrived in the town. When they saw that the British had three times as many soldiers, they headed back to Concord. They positioned themselves where they could not be seen, in order to observe the British movements. As they watched and waited, more militia men joined them.

The British divided into smaller groups of **sentries** and search parties. They searched the town of Concord for weapons, but found only a small number of them. The townspeople directed the searchers away from the main supply of weapons that had been buried in a local farmer's field.

What Do You Think?

If you were a townsperson in Concord, would you have lied to the British to help the Patriots? Why or why not?

Battle of Concord

The Patriots Assemble

Meanwhile, as the number of militia grew, Barrett moved them to surround the British soldiers searching Concord's North Bridge. Some of the British troops began firing as they tried to defend their position, but they were outnumbered and in a bad position. Fourteen soldiers were killed in the fight. The rest of the soldiers quickly abandoned their position and retreated to the town center.

The Redcoats Retreat

> *I wish this cursed place was burned.*
>
> —British General Thomas Gage, writing about Boston in 1775

Barrett's troops moved back to their previous position at the edge of town and waited. When Colonel Smith ordered his British troops to march back to Boston, the Patriot militia fired on them while hiding behind stone walls, trees, barns, and houses. This was very effective since British soldiers were not used to fighting in the wilderness against snipers. British **casualties** were nearly 300 dead, wounded, or missing. The colonists' confidence rose dramatically. As they neared Boston, the Redcoats were running and had to be rescued by fellow British soldiers. The next morning, the British awoke to a militia army of about 20,000.

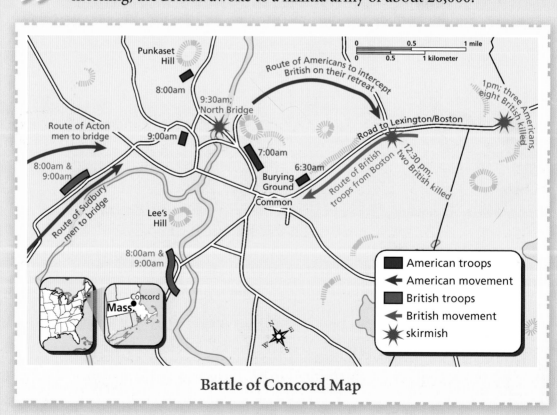

Battle of Concord Map

The Battle of Bunker (Breed's) Hill

The British were **confined** to Boston following the battles of Lexington and Concord. The Patriot militia had no navy, but they controlled the only land access to Boston. The British had access to sea routes and used its navy ships to provide new supplies whenever they were needed. British **reinforcements** arrived throughout the month of May.

> *It was on the seventeenth, by break of day,*
> *The Yankees did surprise us,*
> *With their strong works they had thrown up,*
> *To burn the town and drive us. . . .*
> *"Bad luck to him [General Howe] by land and sea,*
> *For he's despis'd by many;*
> *The name of Bunker Hill he dreads,*
> *Where he was flogg'd most plainly..*
>
> —"Battle of Bunker Hill" poem by a British Officer

What Do You Know!

The muskets used in the Revolutionary War were flintlocks, meaning that a trigger would create sparks on a piece of flint to ignite the gunpowder. They were loaded from the muzzle, or shooting end, of the gun. They weighed about 20 pounds (9 kg). They could shoot up to 175 yards (160 m) away but were not always accurate.

British Strategy

British Generals William Howe, John Burgoyne and Henry Clinton arrived in late May. The generals began planning to retake the area around Boston. They planned to first secure the area to the south and then to cross Boston's harbor to the point at Charlestown Heights. This area was a "no man's land" located between the two forces. The British planned to use this area to advance on Cambridge. The initial attack was set for June 18.

During the attack, the British soldiers started to fall rapidly. They eventually retreated and regrouped for another **assault** on the hill. A second march up the hill had the same result and a third push had similar British casualties. However, at that point in the battle—despite their success—the colonists were forced to retreat towards Charlestown because they had used up almost all of their ammunition and supplies.

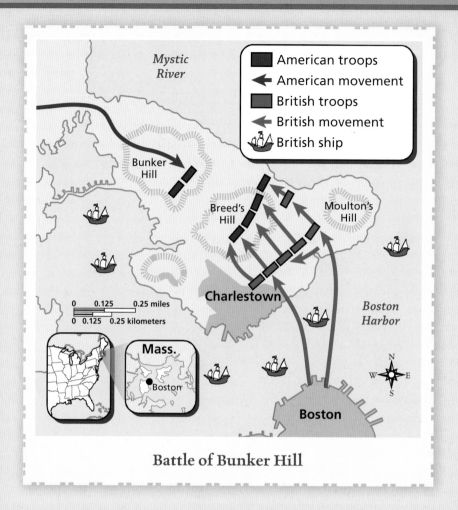

Battle of Bunker Hill

People in the War

Colonel William Prescott

William Prescott was born in Massachusetts in 1726. He was about 50 years old when he led Patriot troops at the Battle of Bunker Hill. In order to save ammunition, he famously told his troops, "Don't fire until you see the whites of their eyes!"

Patriot Tactics

The colonists received word of the coming attack on June 13 and began planning a defense. Colonel William Prescott was ordered to set up positions on Bunker Hill on the Charlestown peninsula. Here the colonists could fire cannons onto the British soldiers in Boston.

On the night of June 16, Colonel Prescott led 1,200 men onto the peninsula and started to build their positions. They intended to build on the larger and better known Bunker Hill. However, they quickly decided to move the work to Breed's Hill, which was lower, but closer to Boston. They built a long, protective wall that was six feet (two meters) tall and had wooden platforms. This allowed the to Patriots shoot over the wall and then take cover behind it.

Results of the Battle

In the early morning, the British saw the extent of the Patriots' work done overnight and began firing cannons on Breed's Hill from the ships in the harbor. This interrupted work on the Patriot's **fortifications,** but did not stop it.

That afternoon General Gage ferried British troops across the harbor to attack the hill. The Patriots were low on ammunition and far away from the landing site, so they did not fire on the British as they landed. As British troops attacked the fortified hill, however, they suffered more than 1,150 casualties—nearly half their force. Patriot casualties numbered only 450 by comparison. Although the colonists eventually lost the battle, they had new confidence that they could effectively fight the powerful British army **regulars**.

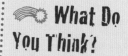

What Do You Think?

Losing a battle usually makes troops feel bad. Why did losing the battle that took place on Breed's Hill make the Patriots feel confident?

Bunker Hill illustration

The Siege of Boston

The Siege of Boston began in April 1775 and lasted until March 1776. Following the battles of Lexington and Concord, patriot militia forces closed in around the city of Boston. This limited the British troops' movements to the city of Boston. After the battle of Bunker Hill, neither side gained any significant ground. There were minor **skirmishes,** but no other large battles.

British Forces Withdraw

On July 3, 1775, General George Washington was given command of the newly established Continental Army. His goal was to force the British to leave Boston by bombarding the British ships bringing in fresh supplies. Over the winter, Washington brought cannons that were captured at Fort Ticonderoga to the Boston area. He positioned the cannons in nearby Dorchester Heights, overlooking Boston. From there, Washington's men bombarded both the town of Boston and the British fleet. The British attempted to return cannon fire from their ships but could not reach the Patriots' position.

The British commander, William Howe, realized it would be more and more difficult to maintain British control of Boston. Instead he chose to withdraw, and evacuated over 11,000 British troops by ship. They departed on March 17 for Halifax, Nova Scotia, in Canada.

Siege of Boston

16

The Battle of Quebec

In September 1775, Washington's Continental Army began moving north from Boston to Quebec, Canada. Their goal was to free Quebec from British control. On the way, Brigadier General Richard Montgomery led a **regiment** along Lake Champlain and successfully captured Fort St. Jean and Montreal. Colonel Benedict Arnold led another regiment of 1,100 men through the wilderness of Maine toward the city of Quebec.

What Do You Know!

The land of Quebec was settled as part of New France in the mid-1600s. The name Quebec comes from the Algonquin word meaning "where the river narrows." Quebec became a British colony in 1763 after the French and Indian War. Quebec is now an eastern province of Canada, and about half of Quebec's 7 million people are of French ancestry.

A British Victory

Montgomery and Arnold made plans to lead attacks from opposite sides of Quebec at the same time. Montgomery attacked Quebec during a heavy snowstorm on December 30, 1775. He was immediately killed in the battle along with his two chief officers. The remaining officers ordered a withdrawal, and most of the Patriots were either killed or wounded. Unaware of Montgomery's death, Arnold led an attack on the other side of the town. The attack was **repelled** and Arnold was injured in the fighting.

Arnold attempted to storm the city again, but he did not have enough supplies. The British had all of the supplies they needed for the winter. In May 1776, the British fleet delivered 4,000 new troops, and the Patriots retreated to New York.

Benedict Arnold was injured at the Battle of Quebec.

The Fight for the Middle Colonies

Major Events

1776

War spreads to Mid-Atlantic Colonies

August 27
Battle of Long Island

December 26
Battle of Trenton

1777

January 4
Battle of Princeton

September–October
Battles of Saratoga

While the American Revolution broke out in New England, fierce fighting happened in the Middle Colonies as well. These battles included New York City, Ticonderoga, and Saratoga in New York and Trenton, and Princeton in New Jersey.

Battles for New York

Following their retreat from Boston, the British did not control any major territories in the colonies. The British saw New York as a key strategic area and wanted to recapture it. This would cut off communication and supplies between the northern and southern colonies. In June, the British sailed from Halifax, Canada, under General William Howe. By mid-August, they had over 32,000 troops on Staten Island, and over 15,000 British troops on Long Island.

Fortunately, General Washington expected this military tactic. He ordered his army troops to leave Boston and move to New York. His strategy was to prevent the British navy from moving up the Hudson River. Once they reached New York, Washington's men prepared a defense position at the top of the hills in Brooklyn Heights.

American troops and their equipment retreated by ship from Long Island to Manhattan.

NATIVE AMERICANS AND THE REVOLUTIONARY WAR

Native Americans fought for both sides during the American Revolution. Some allied with the British, who helped fight against the French in the French and Indian War. This included the Iroquois, Mohawk, Seneca, Cayuga, Wyandot, and Onondaga nations. Other nations, like the Oneidas and Tuscaroras, sided with the Patriots to avoid fighting alongside their long-time Native American enemies. Both the British and the Patriot armies recruited Native Americans to act as scouts and to help defend the forts.

One important ally for the British was Joseph Brant, a Mohawk chief. Family connections helped Brant join the British Army. Brant was commissioned as a captain and visited Great Britain in 1775, on the eve of war.

Brant led four of the six Iroquois nations in battle for the British. He and his troops fought on the frontiers of New York and Pennsylvania. After the war, Brant helped Native Americans on the frontier make peace with the United States. He later settled in Ontario on a grant of land from Great Britain.

Retreating from the British

After the Continental Army's escape, General Washington had fortifications built to defend his position. Rain during this time held off further British attacks. As the rain began to clear, Washington realized his position could not be defended and it was time to withdraw. During the night of August 29, 1776, Washington's troops withdrew across the East River to Manhattan under cover of darkness, fog, and bad weather.

 The Action at Brooklyn Heights

The British spent five days preparing to attack the Patriot positions at Brooklyn Heights. Howe learned that one Patriot **flank** was weak, so he sent troops there. When the British attacked, the Patriots found themselves with opponents in front, beside, and behind them. The Patriots were in a hopeless battle.

A small group of militiamen from Maryland and Delaware held off the British troops for as long as possible. Almost all of these militiamen were killed or captured. However, their efforts allowed the rest of the army to escape.

The next morning, the British charged Brooklyn Heights but found only empty trenches. The British could have won a more decisive victory, but General Howe ordered his troops not to pursue the Patriots as they retreated. He wanted to avoid another battle like Bunker Hill, where he had lost nearly 1,000 soldiers. Eventually Howe's troops drove the Patriot army out of New York and into New Jersey.

The Battle of Trenton

Patriot troops had lost confidence after a series of defeats in New York. General Washington came up with a plan to boost their **morale** before the end of the year. On the night of December 25, 1776, he and his men crossed the icy Delaware River. Then they marched nine miles (15 km) and split into two groups to attack an enemy post at Trenton, New Jersey.

Caught Off Guard

The British army hired professional German soldiers—called Hessians—to help them fight the Patriots. The Hessians were responsible for protecting the British post at Trenton. Since it was Christmas night, the Hessians thought they were safe from attack. They were asleep when Washington's troops attacked them from both sides. They put up a very small fight and quickly surrendered their entire force and a large number of arms and ammunition. This was a major victory for the Patriot troops' morale, and rekindled their determination to continue fighting in the war.

General Washington leading his troops across the Delaware.

> *... use the bayonet. I am resolved to take Trenton.*
>
> —General George Washington, prior to the surprise attack on Trenton, December 26, 1776

The British Army Responds

General Howe ordered a **counterattack** when he learned of the defeat in Trenton. On January 2, 1777, General Lord Cornwallis marched 6,000 British troops to Trenton to fight the Patriots. Washington's army was outnumbered, but they fought back several British attempts to overtake the bridge into town.

Fooled Again

Cornwallis decided to wait until morning to attack again, against the advice of his officers. During the night, Washington arranged for a few men to keep the campfires burning, and to make **entrenchment** noises. Moving very quietly, the rest of Washington's army moved through the woods around the British forces and toward Princeton. Cornwallis began his attack on Trenton at dawn on January 3 but found that the Patriots were gone.

Aid from Abroad

Vital support for the American Revolutionary War efforts came from France, Spain, and the Netherlands.

1776–1778: France gave the American government loans, money, and weapons.

1778: France and America signed a treaty of alliance. After this, France provided the Patriots with troops and warships.

1779: Spain entered the war as an ally of France.

1780: The Netherlands provided muskets and money to the Americans.

The Hessians at Trenton

Battle of Princeton

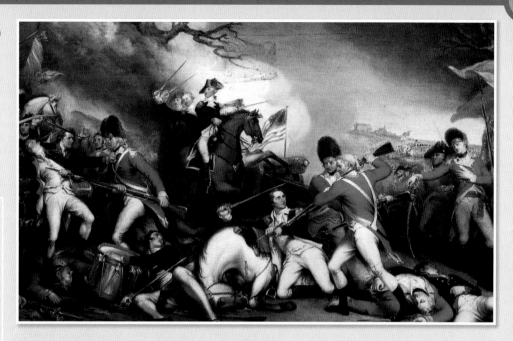

I am just moving to Morristown where I shall endeavor to put [the troops] under the best cover I can . . .

—George Washington to Congress, January 5, 1777

The Battle of Princeton

As the Patriots arrived in Princeton, they split into groups to form an attack. The group led by General Mercer was sent to guard the left flank. They ran into British troops led by Colonel Mawhood and immediately began to fight. Mercer was killed in the charge, and the British side suffered heavy casualties. Patriot reinforcements began arriving and forced the British troops to retreat. Some of Mawhood's troops fled to the town of Princeton, where they were quickly surrounded and forced to surrender.

Washington pursued the rest of Mawhood's troops that went east toward New Brunswick, Canada. However, Washington quickly turned back toward Princeton to avoid Cornwallis's troops returning from Trenton. Washington gathered his men as he went through Princeton and continued on to Morristown, New Jersey, for the winter. The British moved on to their base in New Brunswick to avoid further fighting in **rural** areas. This effectively removed any British presence in New Jersey, which demonstrated that the Patriots were capable of fighting the powerful British army. Politically, it also helped France and Spain decide to take sides with America by providing military and financial support.

The Battle of Ticonderoga

Fort Ticonderoga was strategically located on the route from the Hudson River in New York to British-controlled Canada. It was captured by the Patriots in 1775 under the Patriot leadership of Ethan Allen and Benedict Arnold. Later, George Washington ordered the fort's cannons to be moved to Boston, where he could use them to attack the British navy. Fort Ticonderoga was not maintained after that and fell into disrepair.

Then in early 1777, American General Arthur St. Clair received orders to retake Fort Ticonderoga. The plan was to use the fort to house weapons and supplies throughout the winter months, and to protect the northern colonies from British attacks.

Bombarding the Fort and an Abrupt Withdrawal

Also in early 1777, the British government began preparations for a new advance on New York. British forces, under General John Burgoyne, traveled south from Canada along Lake Champlain to Fort Ticonderoga. They brought cannons up the surrounding mountains and fired on the fort below. While the fort's defensive structure had been improved, it was no match for the cannon fire from above.

General St. Clair saw that his position would be almost impossible to defend. On the night of July 6, 1777, he evacuated the fort under cover of darkness. He moved his troops south to join up with the rest of the Continental Army. This allowed Burgoyne's British forces to occupy Fort Ticonderoga again. St. Clair's abrupt retreat caused furious outrage among the colonies. He spent the rest of his life justifying his actions.

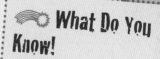

What Do You Know!

GREEN MOUNTAIN BOYS
Ethan Allen was the leader of the Green Mountain Boys, an improvised group of militiamen stationed to defend the frontier of what is now Vermont. The Green Mountain Boys fought for the Patriots during the Revolutionary War. Less than a hundred of them were able to capture Fort Ticonderoga in 1775.

> *The shameful abandonment of Ticonderoga [by the Americans] has not been equalled in the history of the world.*
>
> —Reverend Thomas Allen, July 1777

Turning Point: Saratoga

Burgoyne's capture of Fort Ticonderoga was the first stage in the British plan to split the colonies. The next step was to confuse the Patriots with an unusual means of attack. British Colonel St. Leger was to bring his troops down the Mohawk River from Lake Erie. Meanwhile, General Clinton was to move his troops up from New York to meet Burgoyne. Then Burgoyne and Clinton would surprise the Continental Army as they fought St. Leger's troops.

Led by General Horatio Gates, the Patriots established a position at Bemis Heights, New York. The second in command was General Benedict Arnold. The cautious Gates and aggressive Arnold did not agree on their **strategy.** Arnold urged Gates to attack as soon as Burgoyne's army arrived below Bemis Heights. Gates preferred to defend their position from the hilltop.

> *I am, with real affection and esteem, dear General [Gates], your obedient, humble servant . . .*
>
> —Benedict Arnold to General Horatio Gates, August 31, 1776

Action at the Battle of Freeman's Farm

On September 19, 1777, Burgoyne arrived ahead of Clinton and began to move his troops onto Freeman's farm. Gates eventually allowed Arnold to take a **division** to meet the British. Arnold's men attacked in waves and began to overwhelm Burgoyne's men. A German regiment, fighting for the British, came around the battlefield to assist. Gates refused to let his troops join the fight. As a result, Arnold's troops had to withdraw to the Patriot position atop Bemis Heights.

Burgoyne's men took heavy losses in the fighting, so he waited for Clinton's army to arrive. Clinton, however, was not making progress moving up the Hudson River. Burgoyne eventually realized Clinton would take too long to arrive.

People in the War

General Horatio Gates

Horatio Gates was born in England in 1728. He fought in the French and Indian War as a major in the British army. He moved to what is now West Virginia after that war. Gates oversaw the fighting in Saratoga and was elected president of the Board of War. However, he suffered a bad defeat in South Carolina by Lord Cornwallis. After the war, Gates moved to New York and became a state representative.

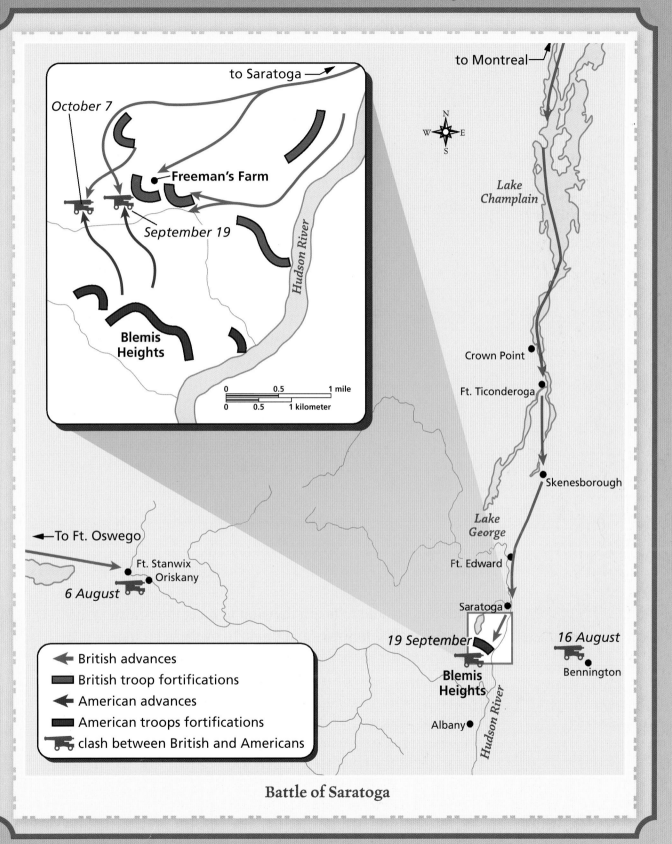

to Montreal

October 7

to Saratoga

Freeman's Farm

September 19

Lake Champlain

Blemis Heights

Hudson River

0   0.5   1 mile
0   0.5   1 kilometer

Crown Point

Ft. Ticonderoga

Skenesborough

Lake George

To Ft. Oswego

Ft. Stanwix
Oriskany

6 August

Ft. Edward

Saratoga

19 September

16 August

Blemis Heights

Bennington

Albany

Hudson River

British advances
British troop fortifications
American advances
American troops fortifications
clash between British and Americans

Battle of Saratoga

Major General
Benedict Arnold

General Washington realized a major battle was shaping up. He encouraged all militia and colonists in the area to help the Continental Army in any way they could. By the time the fighting resumed, the Patriots had about 12,000 men. The British had only about 4,000 troops and had suffered heavy casualties. At the Patriot camp, Gates and Arnold continued to disagree. Eventually, Gates stripped Arnold of his command.

Action at Bemis Heights

On October 7, Burgoyne assembled troops to try to occupy a hill to the west of the Patriot position. Arnold's men, now under General Simon Fraser, moved to attack the British troops. When Fraser was killed in the battle, Arnold jumped back in to take command. He rallied the Patriots to victory over the outnumbered British and German troops. Arnold was badly wounded in the fighting when his horse fell on his leg and broke it.

Burgoyne was forced to withdraw British troops back to Saratoga. The Continental Army followed Burgoyne and surrounded his camp at Saratoga. On October 17, Burgoyne realized he was badly outnumbered and had no escape route. Just like all British leaders, he and Clinton were accustomed to planning attacks out in the open in Europe. Fighting in the wilderness required more sophisticated communications and more time to travel through rugged land. Both Burgoyne and Clinton underestimated these complications. By splitting up their armies, they could not lead a unified attack. When Burgoyne realized Clinton's army would not arrive in time, he surrendered his army to General Gates.

> ### 🌠 What Do You Think?
>
> Was General Gates right to remove General Arnold because they disagreed on the battle strategy? Why or why not?

The Impact of Saratoga

Burgoyne's surrender at Saratoga meant Britain lost a quarter of its troops in North America. It also meant Britain failed to take control of the northern and middle colonies. This proved that the Continental Army was capable of competently fighting the British. It also encouraged support for America from Europe. When word arrived in France, negotiations for an alliance between France and the United States began almost immediately. Later, Spain—an ally of France—would also support America.

> *I have been surrounded with enemies, ill-treated by pretended friends, abandoned by a considerable part of my own army . . . under perpetual fire, and exhausted with laborious days, and 16 almost sleepless nights, without change of clothes, or other covering than the sky. I have been with my army within the jaws of famine; shot through my hat and waistcoat, my nearest friends killed round me; and from these combined misfortunes and escapes, I imagine I am reserved to stand a war with ministers who will always lay the blame upon the employed who miscarries.*
>
> —Major-General Burgoyne to his nieces, October 20, 1777

The Surrender of General Burgoyne

Pennsylvania & Valley Forge

General Howe was unable to draw Washington's Continental Army back to the New Jersey area, so he planned to capture Philadelphia, the capital of the colonies. This was why Howe did not actively support Burgoyne at Saratoga. He believed it was more important to capture the seat of the colonial government.

The Fight for Philadelphia

In August 1777, Howe moved 15,000 troops by boat from New York to the north end of Chesapeake Bay. Then they began a march toward Philadelphia. On September 9, Washington positioned 11,000 Patriot soldiers in their path at Brandywine Creek. This was his best opportunity to prevent the British from reaching Philadelphia. General Howe sent a portion of his men on a long march around the Patriot position. On September 11, Howe attacked from the side and behind the Patriot positions. The Patriots took heavy losses and had to retreat.

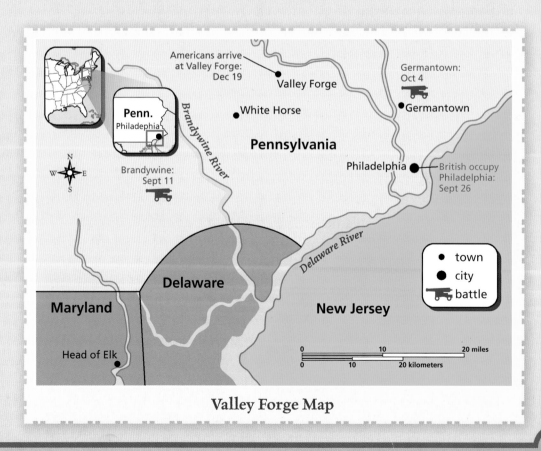

Valley Forge Map

Surprises on Both Sides

Howe's position made a Patriot retreat to Philadelphia impossible. This left the colonies' capital largely undefended, and the Continental Congress immediately evacuated Philadelphia. Fifteen days later, on September 26, the British marched into Philadelphia unopposed. This did not have the effect the British had hoped, since the American government was no longer there.

The British set up camp for about 9,000 of their men at Germantown, about five miles (8 km) north of Philadelphia. Washington drew up a plan to attack Germantown early in the morning. The attack began early on October 4. The advancing Patriots were spotted by British sentries. The sentries fired their **rifles**, and the surprise was lost. There were heavy casualties on both sides, but the Patriot attack was repelled.

There were minor skirmishes following the attack, but no major battles that fall. Washington brought Patriot troops to Valley Forge for the winter. He realized that his men were brave, but unskilled. He spent six winter months at Valley Forge training his troops for the next year.

> *You are mistaken; it is not the British army that has taken Philadelphia, but Philadelphia that has taken the British army.*
>
> —The Chevalier de Pontgibaud, describing the British army's surprise when discovering the Continental Congress had evacuated Philadelphia, 1777

The Camp and Conditions at Valley Forge

Starting in November 1777, an extremely harsh winter fell on Valley Forge. The living conditions were terrible. Approximately 12,000 Patriot soldiers built more than a thousand huts to provide some protection from the cold. Soldiers did not receive adequate supplies of food, and their clothes were in very bad condition. Many soldiers did not even have shoes or blankets. The snow and ice would freeze and melt repeatedly. This made it impossible to keep dry. The conditions were ideal for disease. Pneumonia, typhoid, frostbite, and starvation were common. Over 2,500 men died from disease, starvation, or exposure over the winter.

Von Steuben at Valley Forge

What Do You Think?

How was the winter at Valley Forge both good and bad for the Patriots?

People in the War

Baron von Steuben

Frederich William von Steuben, was born in what is now north central Germany in 1730. He became a soldier at age 16. He was well known for his military ability by the time the American Revolution began. He was very enthusiastic about the Patriot cause and came to Valley Forge in February 1778 to train the Continental Army. Steuben lived extravagantly in New York after the war until his death in 1794.

In February 1778, Baron von Steuben—a former leader of the **Prussian** army—arrived to train Washington's men at Valley Forge. Steuben taught the Patriots military skills and discipline, and made them into a strong, forceful, and confident army. This, in addition to overcoming great hardship that winter, improved morale dramatically and helped the Continental Army emerge from Valley Forge as a toughened force capable of defeating the British.

> *[Baron von Steuben's] knowledge in Discipline is very great, his method of maneuvering is very Difficult…*
>
> —Ezra Selden, Captain in the First Connecticut Regiment, describing the training at Valley Forge, May 15, 1778

Supplies and assistance for the Continental Army also began to arrive from France. Howe feared that the French navy would cut off his connection to British supplies. In the spring of 1778, the British army left Philadelphia to return to New York.

3. The War at Sea

The sea was a key method of transport and communication in the 1700s. Ships were used to transport troops, food, ammunition, clothes, and other goods of daily life. The British Royal navy was a dominant military force in the world at that time, but it had begun to lose its prominence before the American Revolution. It did not have enough ships in good repair to patrol the long American coastline.

Privateers Support the Patriots

During the first three years of the war, the British navy was mostly used to transport troops and supplies in support of the army. The Patriots, however, did not have a navy at the beginning of the war. Instead, they made use of privateers. These were privately owned ships that were given permission by Congress to attack and capture British ships and their cargo.

The privateers would then sell whatever they captured and keep the money. This caused major supply problems for the British. John Adams (who later became president of the United States) wrote: "It is by cutting off supplies, not by attacks, sieges, or assaults that I expect deliverance from enemies."

Major Events

1775
Continental Navy created, commanded by Commodore Esek Hopkins

1778
HMS *Drake* captured by Continental Navy

April
French send 16 ships to support Patriots

Spring
British evacuate Philadelphia

1779
HMS *Serapis* captured by Continental Navy

1781

September
Royal Navy is prevented from reaching Cornwallis's army

October 9
British surrender at Battle of Yorktown

Esek Hopkins

The Continental Navy

In 1775, the Continental Congress authorized the formation of the Continental Navy, commanded by Commodore Esek Hopkins. It was inexperienced and limited to raiding British controlled ports for supplies. It could not compete with the larger British ships. The most successful captain of that time was John Paul Jones, a Scotsman who joined the Continental Navy. He was able to capture the HMS *Drake* in 1778, and the larger HMS *Serapis* the following year. He even led raids on British ports in England. This caused concern in Great Britain, and weakened support for the war.

🌠 What Do You Know!

WARSHIPS OF THE LATE 18TH CENTURY

The main warship of the 18th century was called the **ship of the line**. These were huge sailing ships that were powerful enough to withstand battle. The most common size had 74 cannons on board, with 37 cannons on each side.

Since these large ships were not very easy to maneuver, they fought using an effective naval tactic called the "line of battle." Two columns of opposing battleships arranged themselves so one line of ships had cannons facing an opposing line of ships' cannons. This tactic allowed the ships on either side to fire as many cannons as possible, all at once, at their enemy.

Smaller, faster ships, known as **frigates**, were used as scouts for the fleet. They would investigate the path ahead and relay information to the larger warships.

Frigate

France Supports America at Sea

The French were also rebuilding their navy at this time. After forming an alliance with the Americans, France lent military support to the colonies. This naval support had a major impact on the war. In April 1778, France sent 16 ships to North America. News of the French fleet caused British troops to evacuate Philadelphia in the spring of 1778.

> *There are between thirty and forty sail within the capes, most of them ships of war and some of them very big.*
>
> —General Lord Cornwallis, reporting to General Clinton on the arrival of the French fleet at Yorktown, 1781

Three years later, the French navy helped secure America's success in the American Revolution by winning the greatest naval victory of the war. In the summer of 1781, General Lord Cornwallis's British army arrived in Yorktown, Virginia, and waited for the Royal Navy to transport his troops to New York. Since Yorktown had access to Chesapeake Bay, Washington quickly realized the strategic importance of the bay. He asked the French fleet to take control of the bay and prevent Cornwallis from escaping.

In September 1781, the French fleet, led by Admiral de Grasse, arrived in the Chesapeake with 27 ships of the line and engaged the Royal Navy in battle at sea. By drawing the British fleet away from the Chesapeake, the French prevented the British fleet from resupplying or rescuing Cornwallis's army. This contributed to a defeat of the British army at Yorktown, which ultimately led to American independence.

What Do You Think?

Why was it important for Washington to plan ahead when involving the French Navy in his military strategy?

Line of Battle

> *...the victory in the end was to the holder of the sea line of communications.*
>
> —British historian Captain W. M. James, on the Battle of the Chesapeake's pivotal role in winning the American Revolution

The South and Yorktown

Major Events

1778

December 1778– October 1779
Savannah captured by the British

1780

May 12, 1780
Charleston captured by the British

1781

January 17
Battle of Cowpens

March 15
Battle of Guilford Courthouse

October 9
Battle of Yorktown; Britain surrenders, effectively ending the war

1783

September 3
Treaty of Paris; formal end of the war

While New England and the Middle Colonies saw their share of fighting during the American Revolution, the end of the war came in the Southern colony of Virginia. Virginia and the Southern colonies saw significant fighting, particularly on the coast.

Savannah and Charleston Seized

When France blocked British forces from resupplying their weapons and troops in the Northern colonies, the British turned their attention to the Southern colonies. They felt the South would offer less resistance than the North. Not only was the number of pro-British Loyalists greater in the South, but southern Loyalists were also more inclined to defend their cause with guns and knives. In addition, Britain offered freedom to any slave who fought for them, and many took up the offer.

Savannah Falls to the British

In December 1778, a British army of over 3,000 moved to the outskirts of Savannah, Georgia, under the command of Colonel Mark Prevost. They easily outnumbered the less than 1,000 Patriot troops, and the British claimed a victory in Savannah. By 1779, all of Georgia was under British control.

In the fall of 1779, French Admiral d'Estaing brought 4,000 French troops to Georgia. He and American General Benjamin Lincoln attempted to recapture Savannah. Prevost's troops successfully defended Savannah in a one-sided battle. Lincoln and d'Estaing abandoned their siege.

Charleston Falls to the British

In the spring of 1780, Sir Henry Clinton led a combined expedition of over 14,000 British army and navy troops to take Charleston. Clinton set up a navy **blockade** around Charleston's harbor. Then he used the army to surround Charleston and began **bombarding** the city with cannon fire. Lincoln was badly outnumbered and cut off from support. The Patriots surrendered Charleston to the British on May 12.

Siege of Charleston

The Battles in the Carolinas

After the fall of Charleston, there was little resistance remaining in the South. British command in the South passed to General Lord Cornwallis. The Continental Congress sent General Horatio Gates to lead the Patriot counterattack.

Gates attempted an attack on the British position at Camden, South Carolina, in the early morning of August 16, 1780. Much of Gates's army included untrained militia. They were rapidly defeated, and many of the militiamen retreated. Gates went with them, destroying his reputation as a military commander. The remaining soldiers fought well, but they were outnumbered and lost to the British.

An Upstart Southern Leader for the Patriots

General Greene

Gates was replaced by General Nathanael Greene. Greene had experience in both military tactics and in keeping an army supplied. He rebuilt the Continental Army in the South and planned an unusual strategy to take on the larger British forces. He used small groups of men to fight small battles with the British in places further and further away from the British base. This would stretch the British supply lines to the breaking point.

Greene sent 800 of his men west under General Daniel Morgan hoping to draw the British out. This succeeded. The British attacked Greene's troops at Cowpens, North Carolina, on January 17, 1781. Greene's men pretended to retreat in panic from the larger British force, but they regrouped behind the next hill. The British charged into Morgan's trap and were defeated.

> *We fight, get beat, rise, and fight again. . . .*
>
> —General Nathanael Greene, 1781

General Lord Cornwallis Responds

Cornwallis was shocked by the defeat. He immediately set out to attack the Patriots at Cowpens. The Patriots, however, had already left. Cornwallis discarded his supply wagons and anything else that was slowing down his exhausted troops in order to chase Greene's army.

Battle of Cowpens

Cornwallis believed that defeating Greene could lead to the end of the war in the South. However, Greene was on home turf and knew the area well. He stayed ahead of Cornwallis and prepared a stand at Guilford Courthouse, North Carolina.

On March 15, 1781, Greene's 1,900 soldiers faced 4,000 British regulars under Cornwallis. After a long and bloody battle, Greene's army withdrew, but Cornwallis lost one-third of his troops. He made every attempt to catch the retreating Patriots, but each day his supplies ran shorter while Greene's army gained strength. Cornwallis abandoned the chase and moved toward Virginia, which was the main source of supplies for the Patriots. His goal was to cut off the flow of Patriot supplies from Virginia to North Carolina while also joining forces with General Phillips's 3,500 British troops.

Greene's army moved South and continued to cause problems for the British. They made a series of attacks on British positions and eventually forced the British to withdraw to Charleston.

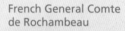

What Do You Think?

Brilliant military strategy often means taking risks by doing something unexpected. How did the element of surprise help General Greene's troops?

Endgame: Yorktown

Once in Virginia, General Lord Cornwallis established a British base at Yorktown. He chose this location on the order of his superior, Henry Clinton. Yorktown was a deep-water port, capable of receiving large ships that could resupply Cornwallis with fresh troops and supplies. Clinton promised that reinforcements and supplies would be sent from New York, so Cornwallis moved his entire force to Yorktown. This would prove to be a fateful decision.

In 1781, American General George Washington and French General Comte de Rochambeau met in New York and agreed to work together. Their plan was to make the British think they intended to attack Clinton's position in New York. Instead they moved south to attack Yorktown. They were supported by the French navy led by Admiral Comte de Grasse. The combined armies arrived in Yorktown on September 28 and immediately surrounded the town.

French General Comte de Rochambeau

The Noose Tightens and Cornwallis Surrenders

General Lord Cornwallis expected to receive support from the Royal Navy. However, the French fleet blocked the British ships from reaching Yorktown earlier that month. Cornwallis was not yet aware that his army was effectively trapped.

While waiting for additional troops to arrive, Cornwallis decided to pull his men back from their outer defensive positions. These positions were rapidly taken up by the Patriots and the French. The allies dug **trenches** from there to get even closer to the British position. By October 9, they had many cannons in place and began firing. The bombardment continued for a week as the Patriots and the French moved closer and closer to the British fort.

☄ Siege at Yorktown

Siege warfare was common at the time. A siege involves surrounding a town or fort. The defenders have no way to escape or get supplies. Typically they give up from lack of food rather than direct attack.

In the case of Yorktown, the town was surrounded on land by the Patriot and French armies. The river and sea accesses were cut off by the French navy. The British could be attacked from all sides. As American and French cannons got closer, the British sustained more and more damage.

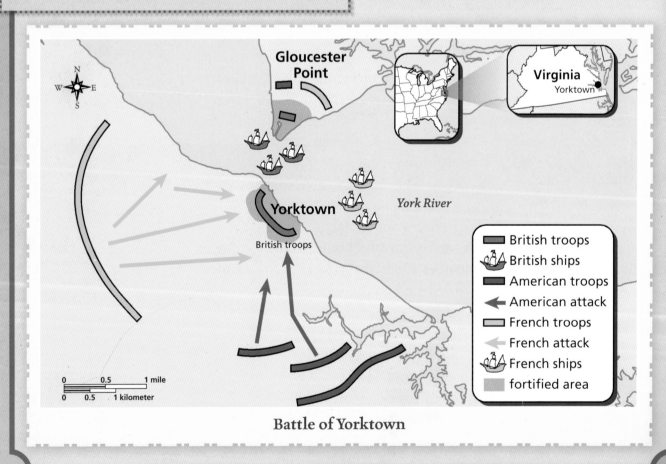

Battle of Yorktown

Surrender at Yorktown

🌠 **What Do You Know!**

In the 1700s, the head of the army would turn over his sword in order to surrender. Contrary to this tradition, General Cornwallis did not turn over his sword to George Washington. Cornwallis sent an aide with his sword instead.

On the morning of October 16, Cornwallis attempted to evacuate his troops across the river, but a storm made the crossing impossible. Cornwallis and his officers agreed that their position was hopeless and began negotiations for surrender. The surrender ceremony took place on October 19, 1781.

The surrender at Yorktown marked the end of fighting in the war. Sir Henry Clinton's army in New York was the only major British army left in the colonies. The British did not attempt any other military **campaigns** in America until a peace treaty was signed. Support for the war in Britain dried up as news spread about the British surrender at Yorktown. This led to the signing of the Treaty of Paris in September 1783. That treaty officially ended the war and recognized the independence of the colonies.

> "
> *I have been forced to surrender... the troops under my command... as prisoners of war to the combined forces of America and France.*
>
> —Lt. General Charles Lord Cornwallis, October 20, 1781
> "

After the Battles

The surrender at Yorktown had sealed the fate of the British. Great Britain was used to being the best military and navy in the world. Back in Britain, people were surprised and unhappy that the colonies had defeated the British military. As a result, the government in Parliament changed. A new political party, the Whigs, took over. The Whigs wanted to make peace and end the fighting in America. They knew they could not win.

Shipping Out

At the time of the surrender at Yorktown, there were still 26,000 British troops in America. The troops did not finally leave the new United States until November 25, 1783. This was more than two years after the Battle of Yorktown.

Peace Treaties

The British government and the Continental Congress sent representatives to Paris to make peace. The new United States and Britain had agreed on terms by November 1782. There were, however, other nations involved, specifically France and Spain. Each nation had to make its own peace with Britain. Finally, all of the peace treaties were **ratified** in September 1783. The war was over, and the United States of America was officially an independent nation.

The Revolutionary Flag

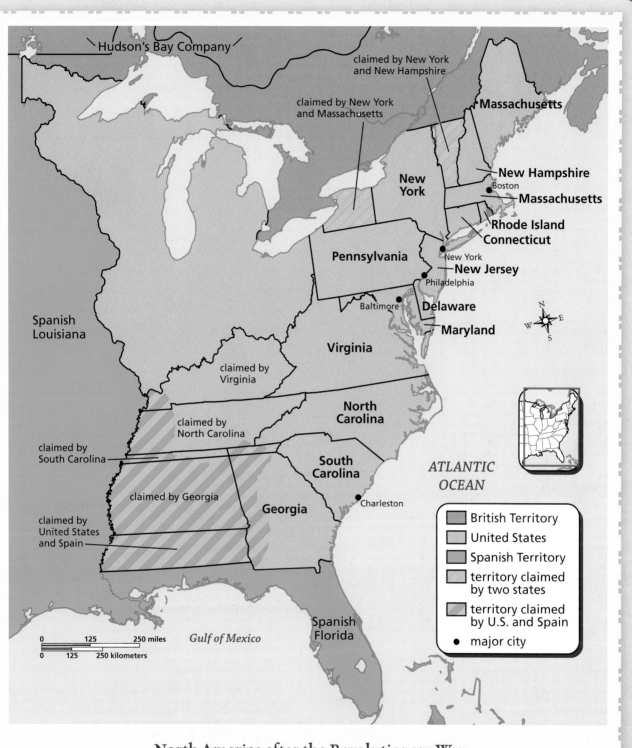

Hudson's Bay Company

claimed by New York
and New Hampshire

claimed by New York
and Massachusetts

Massachusetts

**New
York**

New Hampshire

Boston

Massachusetts

Rhode Island
Connecticut

Pennsylvania

New York

New Jersey

Philadelphia

Spanish
Louisiana

Baltimore

Delaware

Maryland

N
W   E
S

Virginia

claimed by
Virginia

claimed by
North Carolina

**North
Carolina**

claimed by
South Carolina

**South
Carolina**

**ATLANTIC
OCEAN**

claimed by Georgia

Georgia

Charleston

claimed by
United States
and Spain

British Territory

United States

Spanish Territory

territory claimed
by two states

territory claimed
by U.S. and Spain

major city

0   125   250 miles
0   125   250 kilometers

Gulf of Mexico

Spanish
Florida

North America after the Revolutionary War

GLOSSARY

alliance an agreement under which two countries agree to help each other, especially militarily

assault (military) to attack, shoot at, or advance toward an opponent

bayonet a sharp weapon that attaches to the end of a musket; can be used in close fighting

blockade a military tactic in which enemy ships keep goods from coming in or going out of a port

bombard to shoot at, usually with canons

campaign a series of several battles, usually in the same area

casualty someone who is wounded or killed during a battle or attack

confine to keep to a small space or area

confiscate to take away

counterattack to return or fight back against an enemy's attack

division a large unit of an army; during the Revolutionary War, a division was made up of brigades

entrenchment the act of an army building walls (fortifications) or trenches around their position

flank the side of an army's formation; usually a weak part of an army

fortification walls or other construction built around an army to protect their position

frigate a medium-sized ship of war with square sails

harbor a protected area of water deep enough for ships; often the site of a port

militia a small military unit made up of citizens; usually used only in emergency

morale the overall feeling of citizens or an army about accomplishing a task

musket a type of gun loaded from the top; used by Revolutionary War soldiers

Parliament the British government; the representative legislature made up of the House of Lords and House of Commons

privateer a private ship or owner of a private ship hired or authorized for war

Prussia a kingdom in the north of what is now Germany and Poland; known for military strength in the 1700s and 1800s; ruled by the Hohenzollern dynasty

ratify the official approval of a treaty, usually by the whole government of a country

regiment (Continental Army) a military unit made up of 8 companies; volunteers from a specific area served in regiments (i.e. the 2nd New Hampshire Regiment); the Continental Army was supposed to have 27 regiments and a total of 20,000 men

regulars professional soldiers; during the Revolutionary War, primarily British soldiers

reinforcement a regiment or army which comes to back up an attacking or defending army

repel to force back

representative government a system made up of elected leaders who make laws and decisions for the whole country

resistance the act of fighting back; can be active attacks or passive boycotts and other tactics

rifle a type of gun with a long barrel; supposed to be shot from the shoulder

rural countryside or non-developed land; farmland; not urban or city-like

sentry a lookout or guard

ship of the line a very large warship, often difficult to maneuver

siege an army's attack on a city, town, or fort

skirmish a small battle; usually hand-to-hand among few soldiers rather than larger armies

strategy the science of commanding an army; the use of specific tactics in certain situations

surrender to give up or lay down arms

tactics the ways of moving troops and attacking

trench ditches dug to protect troops; ditches used to approach a fortification while protecting from attack

TIMELINE

1775	*April 19*	Battles of Lexington and Concord
	May 10	Siege of Fort Ticonderoga
	May 27	Battle of Chelsea Creek
	June 16–17	Battle of Bunker (Breed's) Hill
	October 13	Continental Congress authorizes the formation of the Continental Navy
	December 31	Battle of Quebec
1776	*July 4*	Declaration of Independence adopted by Continental Congress
	August 27	Battle of Long Island (Brooklyn Heights)
	October 28	Battle of White Plains
	November 16	Battle of Fort Washington
	December 26	Battle of Trenton
1777	*January 3*	Battle of Princeton
	August 16	Battle of Bennington
	September 11	Battle of Brandywine
	September 19	Battle of Saratoga (Freeman's Farm)
	October 4	Battle of Germantown
	October 7	Battle of Saratoga (Bemis Heights)
1778	*June 28*	Battle of Monmouth
	December 29	Capture of Savannah
1780	*March 29*	Siege of Charleston begins
	August 16	Battle of Camden
	October 7	Battle of King's Mountain
1781	*January 17*	Battle of Cowpens
	March 15	Battle of Guilford Courthouse
	September 5	Battle of the Chesapeake (Virginia Capes)
	September 8	Battle of Eutaw Springs
	October 9–19	Battle of Yorktown
1783	*September 3*	Treaty of Paris signed, ending the Revolutionary War

FURTHER READING AND WEBSITES

Books

Aloian, Molly. *George Washington: Hero of the American Revolution*. Crabtree Publishing Company, 2013.

Aloian, Molly. *Phillis Wheatley: Poet of the Revolutionary Era*. Crabtree Publishing Company, 2013.

American Revolution Battles and Leaders. DK Publishing, 2004.

Cocca, Lisa Colozza. *Marquis de Lafayette: Fighting for America's Freedom*. Crabtree Publishing Company, 2013.

Lancaster, Bruce. *The American Heritage History of the American Revolution*. I Books: 2004.

Mason, Helen. *Life on the Homefront during the American Revolution*. Crabtree Publishing Company, 2013.

Perritano, John. *The Causes of the American Revolution*. Crabtree Publishing Company, 2013.

Perritano, John. *The Outcome of the American Revolution*. Crabtree Publishing Company, 2013.

Roberts, Steve. *King George III: England's Struggle to Keep America*. Crabtree Publishing Company, 2013.

Savas, Theodore. and Dameron, David. *A Guide to the Battles of the American Revolution*. Savas Beattie, 2010.

Wood, W. *Battles Of The Revolutionary War: 1775–1781*, Da Capo Press, 2003.

Websites

"The War of the Revolution, 1775 to 1783."
http://www.britishbattles.com/american-revolution.htm

"Major Events of the Revolutionary War."
http://www.historycentral.com/Revolt/battles.html

"The American Revolution (Battles)."
http://www.theamericanrevolution.org/battles.aspx

"Minute Man National Historical Park, Massachusetts."
http://www.nps.gov/mima/index.htm

"Timeline of the Revolutionary War."
http://www.ushistory.org/declaration/revwartimeline.htm

"Yorktown National Battlefield, Virginia."
http://www.nps.gov/yonb/index.htm

BIBLIOGRAPHY

Books

Chadwick, Bruce. *George Washington's War.* Sourcebooks, Inc., 2005.

Lancaster, Bruce. *The American Heritage History of the American Revolution,* I Books, 2004.

Middlekauf, Robert. *The Glorious Cause.* Oxford University Press, 2005.

Werner, Kirk, D. *The American Revolution,* Greenhaven Press, Inc., 2000.

Wood, Gordon, S. *The American Revolution.* The Modern Library, 2002.

Websites

"American Revolution." *Encyclopedia Britannica.*
http://www.britannica.com/EBchecked/topic/617805/American-Revolution

"Minute Man National Historical Park, Massachusetts." *National Park Service.*
http://www.nps.gov/mima/index.htm

"1776–1783: Diplomacy and the American Revolution." *U.S. Department of State Office of the Historian.*
http://history.state.gov/milestones/1776–1783

INDEX

Adams, John, 31
Allen, Ethan, 23
American colonies, 4
Arnold, Colonel Benedict
(US), 17, 23, 24, 26

Blemis Heights (N.Y.), 24–26
Boston, 4–5, 8, 13, 16, 18
Brandywine Creek (Battle of),
28
Brant, Captain Joseph
(Britain), 19
Bunker Hill, Battle of, 5, 13–16
Burgoyne, General John
(Britain), 13, 22, 26–27

Camden (S.C.), Battle of, 35
Canada, 16, 17, 18, 22
causes of Revolutionary War,
4–5
Charleston (S.C.), 5, 34–35
Chesapeake Bay, 28, 33
Clinton, General Sir Henry
(Britain), 13, 24, 26, 35,
37, 39
Concord (Mass.), 9–10, 11–12
Concord (Mass.), Battle of,
11–12
Cornwallis, General Lord
Charles (Britain), 21–22,
33, 35, 36–39
Cowpens (N.C.), Battle of, 36

Dawes, William, 8–9
d'Estaing, Admiral Charles-
Hector, 35

France, 5, 21, 27, 33, 34, 38
Freeman's Farm (N.Y), 24
French and Indian War, 4, 17
French navy, 33, 34
frigate, 32

Gage, General Thomas
(Britain)
9, 12, 15
Gates, General Horatio, 24, 26,
35
George III, King of Great
Britain, 5
Germantown, Battle of, 29
Great Britain, 4, 8
Green Mountain Boys, 23
Greene, General Nathanael
(US),
36–37

Hessian soldiers, 20
HMS *Drake*, 32
HMS *Serapis*, 32
Hopkins, Commodore Esek
(US), 32
Howe, General William
(Britain), 13, 16, 18–19,
21, 28–29

Jones, Captain John Paul (US),
32

Lexington (Mass.), 8–9
Lexington (Mass.), Battle of,
10
Lincoln, General Benjamin, 35

Mawhood, Colonel Charles
(Britain), 22
Mercer, General Hugh (US),
22
Middle Colonies, 18–30
militias, 4
minutemen, 4, 11
Montgomery, Brigadier
General Richard (US), 17
Morgan, General Daniel (US),
36
musket, 13

Native Americans, 19
naval warfare, 5, 31–33
Netherlands, 21
New England, 8–16
New Jersey, 20–22,
New York City, 5, 18, 28, 30
New York, Battle of, (Brooklyn
Heights), 5, 18–19
North Carolina, 36

Parliament, 4
Pennsylvania, 28–29

Index

Philadelphia (Pa.), 5, 28, 30

Pontgibaud, Chevalier de
(France), 29

Prescott, Colonel William
(US), 14

Prevost, Colonel Mark
(Britain), 34

Princeton, Battle of, 18, 22

privateers, 31

Quebec, 17

Quebec, Battle of, 17

representative government, 4

Revere, Paul, 8–9

Rochambeau, General Jean-
Baptist-Donatien, Comte
de, 37

Saratoga, Battle of, 5, 18, 24–
27

Savannah (Ga.), 34–35

ship of the line, 32

South Carolina, 34–36

Southern colonies, 34–39

Spain, 21, 27

St. Clair, General Arthur (US),
23

Steuben, Frederic William,
Baron von, 30

taxes, 4

Ticonderoga, Fort, 18, 23

Treaty of Paris, 39–40

Trenton, Battle of, 5, 18, 20–21

Valley Forge (Pa.), 28–30

Virginia, 37–39

Washington, General George
(US),
16, 18–19, 20–21, 22, 23,
28–29, 33, 37

Yorktown, Battle of, 5, 33, 37–
40